Art Center College of Design
Library
1700 Lida Street
Pasadena, Calif. 91103

PLEASE CHECK FOR 1 CD-ROM in back

BEFORE AND AFTER EACH CIRCULATION

ART CENTER COLLEGE OF DESIGN

mini icons

All rights reserved.

Copyright © book 2003 Pepin van Roojen
Copyright © company logos
Company logos in this book are protected under copyright law. Should you wish to use any of these logos, please consult the relevant company for permission.

The Pepin Press / Agile Rabbit editions
P.O. Box 10349
1001 EH Amsterdam, The Netherlands

Tel +31 20 4202021
Fax +31 20 4201152
mail@pepinpress.com
www.pepinpress.com
www.agilerabbit.com

Concept & series editor: Pepin van Roojen
Icon design: www.twokidsinagarage.com
Layout for this volume: Joost Baardman, Kitty Molenaar

isbn 90 5768 056 4

10 9 8 7 6 5 4 3 2
2007 06 05 04

Manufactured in Singapore

004.0148
M665
2003

mini icons
ミニアイコン ・ 小圖示

Art Center College Library
1700 Lida Street
Pasadena, CA 91103

Graphic Themes & Pictures
90 5768 001 7	1000 Decorated Initials
90 5768 003 3	Graphic Frames
90 5768 007 6	Images of the Human Body
90 5768 012 2	Geometric Patterns
90 5768 014 9	Menu Designs
90 5768 017 3	Classical Border Designs
90 5768 055 6	Signs & Symbols
90 5768 024 6	Bacteria And Other Micro Organisms
90 5768 023 8	Occult Images
90 5768 046 7	Erotic Images & Alphabets
90 5768 062 9	Fancy Alphabets
90 5768 056 4	Mini Icons
90 5768 016 5	Graphic Ornaments (2 CDs)
90 5768 025 4	Compendium of Illustrations (2 CDs)
90 5768 021 1	5000 Animals (4 CDs)

Textile Patterns
90 5768 004 1	Batik Patterns
90 5768 030 0	Weaving Patterns
90 5768 037 8	Lace
90 5768 038 6	Embroidery
90 5768 058 0	Ikat Patterns

Miscellaneous
90 5768 005 x	Floral Patterns
90 5768 052 1	Astrology
90 5768 051 3	Historical & Curious Maps
90 5768 061 0	Wallpaper Designs

Styles (Historical)
90 5768 027 0	Mediæval Patterns
90 5768 034 3	Renaissance
90 5768 033 5	Baroque
90 5768 043 2	Rococo
90 5768 032 7	Patterns of the 19th Century
90 5768 013 0	Art Nouveau Designs
90 5768 060 2	Fancy Designs 1920
90 5768 059 9	Patterns of the 1930s

Styles (Cultural)
90 5768 006 8	Chinese Patterns
90 5768 009 2	Indian Textile Prints
90 5768 011 4	Ancient Mexican Designs
90 5768 020 3	Japanese Patterns
90 5768 022 x	Traditional Dutch Tile Designs
90 5768 028 9	Islamic Designs
90 5768 029 7	Persian Designs
90 5768 036 X	Turkish Designs
90 5768 042 4	Elements of Chinese & Japanese Design

Photographs
90 5768 047 5	Fruit
90 5768 048 3	Vegetables
90 5768 057 2	Body Parts

Web Design
90 5768 018 1	Web Design Index 1
90 5768 026 2	Web Design Index 2
90 5768 045 9	Web Design Index 3
90 5768 063 7	Web Design Index 4

Folding & Packaging
90 5768 039 4	How To Fold
90 5768 040 8	Folding Patterns for Display & Publicity
90 5768 044 0	Structural Package Designs
90 5768 053 x	Mail It!
90 5768 054 8	Special Packaging

More titles in preparation
In addition to the Agile Rabbit series of book+CD-ROM sets, The Pepin Press publishes a wide range of books on art, design, architecture, applied art, and popular culture.

Please visit www.pepinpress.com for more information.

The Pepin Press - Agile Rabbit Editions

Introduction in English	006	pda planning - priority codes	015
Introducción en Español	007	pda planning - symbols	029
Einführung auf deutsch	008	pda planning - miscellaneous	039
Introduzione in Italiano	009	office - people	043
Introduction en français	010	office + computer	049
Introdução em Português	011	business	055
序言（中文版）	012	company logos	059
日本語によるご紹介	013	transport	069
		people	077
		medical + human body	087
		clothing	093
		food + drinks	097
		animals	103
		sports	107
		playing cards	113
		astrology + astronomy	117
		religion	121
		general	127

contents

Art Center College Library
1700 Lida Street
Pasadena, CA 91103

page number

The mini icons in this book are designed for use on hand-held organisers, such as Palm and other PDAs (Personal Digital Assistants). The restrictions dictated by such devices mean that designers must be extremely inventive to produce recognisable images with a minimum of pixels. The resulting designs are of amazing simplicity and must be viewed in small format to be distinguished properly.

This book contains over a thousand mini icons, which can be used as a graphic resource, or inspiration. All the illustrations are stored on the enclosed free CD-ROM (Mac and Windows) and are ready to use for professional quality printed media and web page design. The pictures can also be used to produce postcards – either on paper or digitally – or to decorate your letters, flyers, etc.

They can be imported directly from the CD into most design, image-manipulation, illustration, word-processing and e-mail programs; no installation is required. Some programs will allow you to access the images directly; in others, you will first have to create a document and then import the images. Please consult your software manual for instructions. The names of the files on the CD-ROM correspond with the image numbers in this book. The CD-ROM comes free with this book, but is not for sale separately. The publishers do not accept any responsibility should the CD not be compatible with your system.

For non-professional applications, single images can be used free of charge. The images cannot be used for any type of commercial or other professional application – including all types of printed or digital publications – without prior permission from The Pepin Press/Agile Rabbit Editions.

For inquiries about permissions and fees:
mail@pepinpress.com
Fax +31 20 4201152

page number   english

Los mini iconos incluidos en este libro han sido diseñados para utilizarlos en organizadores portátiles como Palm y otros PDA (Personal Digital Assistants). Debido a las limitaciones que presentan estos aparatos, los diseñadores desarrollan al máximo su inventiva para crear imágenes reconocibles utilizando el menor número de píxeles. Los diseños resultantes son extraordinariamente sencillos y es necesario emplear formatos pequeños para obtener una buena visualización.

Este libro contiene más de un millar de mini iconos que pueden utilizarse como recurso gráfico o simplemente como inspiración. Todas las ilustraciones se encuentran almacenadas en el CD gratuito adjunto (para Mac y Windows) y están listas para su utilización tanto en impresiones profesionales como en el diseño de páginas web. Las imágenes pueden también emplearse para realizar postales, de papel o digitales, o para decorar cartas, folletos, etc.

Estas imágenes se pueden importar desde el CD a la mayoría de programas de diseño, manipulación de imágenes, dibujo, tratamiento de textos y correo electrónico, sin necesidad de utilizar un programa de instalación. Algunos programas le permitirán acceder a las imágenes directamente; otros, sin embargo, requieren la creación previa de un documento para importar las imágenes. Consulte su manual de software en caso de duda.

Los nombres de los archivos almacenados en el CD-ROM corresponden a la numeración de las imágenes utilizada en el libro. El CD-ROM se ofrece de manera gratuita con este libro, pero está prohibida su venta por separado. Los editores no asumen ninguna responsabilidad en el caso de que el CD no sea compatible con su sistema.

Se autoriza el uso de estas imágenes de manera gratuita para aplicaciones no profesionales. No se podrán emplear en aplicaciones de tipo profesional o comercial (incluido cualquier tipo de publicación impresa o digital) sin la autorización previa de The Pepin Press/Agile Rabbit Editions.

Para más información acerca de autorizaciones y tarifas:
mail@pepinpress.com
Fax +31 20 4201152

español　　　　　　　　　　　　　　　　　　　　　　　　page number

Die Miniaturbilder in diesem Buch können auf Handheld-Organizern, wie etwa Palm und anderen PDAs (Personal Digital Assistants) verwendet werden. Die Einschränkungen, die solche Geräte mit sich bringen, verlangen den Designern einen besonderen Einfallsreichtum ab, um gut erkennbare Bilder mit einem Minimum an Pixeln zu entwerfen. Die auf Basis dieser Vorgaben entwickelten Designs sind erstaunlich simpel und müssen, um entsprechend erkennbar zu sein, in einem kleinen Format angezeigt werden.
Dieses Buch enthält mehr als tausend Bilder in Miniaturformat, die als Ausgangsmaterial für grafische Zwecke oder als Anregung genutzt werden können. Alle Abbildungen sind auf der beiliegenden Gratis-CD-ROM (Mac and Windows) gespeichert und lassen sich direkt zum Drucken in professioneller Qualität oder zur Gestaltung von Websites einsetzen.
Sie können sie auch als Motive für Postkarten auf Karton oder in digitaler Form, oder als Ausschmückung für Ihre Briefe, Flyer etc. verwenden.
Die Bilder lassen sich direkt in die meisten Zeichen-, Bildbearbeitungs-, Illustrations-, Textverarbeitungs- und E-Mail-Programme laden, ohne dass zusätzliche Programme installiert werden müssen. In einigen Programmen können die Dokumente direkt geladen werden, in anderen müssen Sie zuerst ein Dokument anlegen und können dann die Datei importieren. Genauere Hinweise dazu finden Sie im Handbuch zu Ihrer Software.
Die Namen der Dateien auf der CD-ROM stimmen mit den Nummern der Bilder in diesem Buch überein. Die CD-ROM wird kostenlos mit dem Buch geliefert und ist nicht separat verkäuflich. Der Verlag haftet nicht für Inkompatibilität der CD-ROM mit Ihrem System.
Für nicht professionelle Anwendungen können einzelne Bilder kostenfrei genutzt werden. Die Bilder dürfen ohne vorherige Genehmigung von The Pepin Press /Agile Rabbit Editions nicht für kommerzielle oder sonstige professionelle Anwendungen einschließlich aller Arten von gedruckten oder digitalen Medien eingesetzt werden.
Für Fragen zu Genehmigungen und Preisen wenden Sie sich bitte an:
mail@pepinpress.com
Fax +31 20 4201152

page number

deutsch

Le mini icone contenute in questo libro sono state ideate per l'utilizzo in palmari, come Palm e altri PDA (Personal Digital Assistant). A causa delle limitazioni che comportano tali dispositivi, i grafici devono sbizzarrirsi al massimo per produrre immagini riconoscibili con un numero minimo di pixel. I disegni che ne risultano sono di una semplicità sorprendente e per distinguerne chiaramente le caratteristiche, devono essere visualizzati in un formato piccolo.

Questo libro comprende più di mille mini icone da utilizzare come risorsa grafica o come fonte di ispirazione. Tutte le illustrazioni sono contenute nel CD-ROM gratuito allegato (per Mac & Windows) e possono essere utilizzate per realizzare stampe di qualità professionale e per la progettazione di pagine Web. Possono essere inoltre usate per creare cartoline, su carta o digitali, o per abbellire lettere, opuscoli, ecc.

Dal CD, le immagini possono essere importate direttamente nella maggior parte dei programmi di grafica, di ritocco, di illustrazione, di scrittura e di posta elettronica; non è richiesto alcun tipo di installazione. Alcuni programmi vi consentiranno di accedere alle immagini direttamente; in altri, invece, dovrete prima creare un documento e poi importare le immagini. Consultate il manuale del software per maggiori informazioni.

I nomi dei file sul CD-ROM corrispondono ai numeri delle immagini riportati in questo libro. Il CD-ROM è allegato al libro gratuitamente e non può essere venduto separatamente. L'editore non può essere ritenuto responsabile qualora il CD non fosse compatibile con il sistema posseduto.

Per applicazioni di tipo non professionale, le singole immagini possono essere utilizzate gratuitamente. Se desiderate utilizzare le immagini per applicazioni di tipo professionale o con scopi commerciali, comprese tutte le pubblicazioni digitali o stampate, sarà necessaria la relativa autorizzazione da parte della casa editrice The Pepin Press/Agile Rabbit Editions.

Per ulteriori informazioni su autorizzazioni e canoni per il diritto di sfruttamento commerciale rivolgetevi a:
mail@pepinpress.com
Fax +31 20 4201152

italiano

Les mini-icônes présentées dans ce livre ont été conçues pour être utilisées dans des organiseurs tels que le Palm et autres assistants numériques personnels (PDA). Vu les restrictions dictées par ce type d'appareil, les concepteurs doivent faire preuve d'une extrême inventivité pour créer des images reconnaissables et d'un nombre de pixels minimal. Au final, ces créations sont d'une extraordinaire simplicité et doivent être visualisées dans un petit format pour les distinguer correctement.

Ce livre contient plus d'un millier de mini-icônes à utiliser comme ressource graphique ou source d'inspiration. Toutes les illustrations, stockées sur le CD-ROM gratuit inclus (pour Mac et Windows), sont prêtes à l'emploi pour la conception de pages Web et de supports imprimés de qualité professionnelle. Elles permettent également de créer des cartes postales, aussi bien sur papier que virtuelles, ou d'agrémenter vos courriers, prospectus et autres.

Vous pouvez les importer directement à partir du CD dans la plupart des applications de création, manipulation graphique, illustration, traitement de texte et messagerie, sans qu'aucune installation ne soit nécessaire. Certaines applications permettent d'accéder directement aux images, tandis que dans d'autres, vous devez d'abord créer un document, puis importer les images. Veuillez consultez les instructions dans le manuel du logiciel concerné.

Les noms des fichiers du CD-ROM correspondent aux numéros des images du livre. Le CD-ROM est fourni gratuitement avec le livre, mais il ne peut être vendu séparément. L'éditeur décline toute responsabilité si ce CD n'est pas compatible avec votre ordinateur.

Vous pouvez utiliser les images individuelles sans frais dans des applications non-professionnelles. Il est interdit d'utiliser les images avec des applications de type professionnel ou commercial (y compris toutes les sortes de publications numériques ou imprimés) sans l'autorisation préalable de The Pepin Press/Agile Rabbit Editions.

Pour tout renseignement relatif aux autorisations et aux frais d'utilisation:
mail@pepinpress.com
Fax +31 20 4201152

page number

français

Os mini-ícones constantes deste livro foram concebidos para utilização em computadores de bolso, como os Palm ou outros PDAs (Personal Digital Assistants). As restrições impostas por este tipo de dispositivos exigem que os designers sejam extremamente criativos para produzirem imagens reconhecíveis com um número mínimo de pixels. Os desenhos resultantes são de uma simplicidade extraordinária e só serão visualizados correctamente num formato de pequenas dimensões.

Este livro contém mais de mil mini-ícones que podem ser usados como recurso gráfico ou inspiração. Todas as ilustrações estão armazenadas no CD-ROM (Mac e Windows) fornecido gratuitamente com o livro, estando prontas para utilização em material impresso de qualidade profissional e na concepção de páginas para a Web. As imagens também podem ser usadas para criar postais, em papel ou digitais, ou para decorar cartas, folhetos, etc. Estas imagens podem ser importadas directamente do CD para a maioria dos programas de desenho, manipulação de imagens, ilustração, processamento de texto e correio electrónico, sem a necessidade de utilizar um programa de instalação. Alguns programas permitirão o acesso directo às imagens, enquanto que noutros será necessário criar um documento antes de importar as imagens. Consulte o manual do software para obter mais informações. Os nomes dos ficheiros no CD-ROM correspondem aos números das imagens indicados no livro.

O CD-ROM é fornecido gratuitamente com o livro, sendo proibido vendê-lo em separado. Os editores não assumem nenhuma responsabilidade no caso de o CD não ser compatível com o seu sistema.

Desde que não seja para aplicação profissional, as imagens individuais podem ser utilizadas gratuitamente. As imagens não podem ser usadas em nenhum tipo de aplicação comercial ou profissional - incluindo todos os tipos de publicações impressas ou digitais - sem a prévia permissão de The Pepin Press/Agile Rabbit Editions.

Para esclarecer dúvidas a respeito das permissões e taxas:
mail@pepinpress.com
Fax +31 20 4201152

português   page number

本書中的那些小圖示係特別設計給掌上型電子萬用手冊使用，諸如 Palm (掌上型電腦) 和其他的 PDA (個人數位助理)。上述裝置之如此嚴格的限制意謂著設計者必須極度發揮其創造力並藉著一最少的圖素來製作可供順利辨識的圖像。製作完成的設計不但擁有令人意想不到的單純性而且必須以能適度區別之小格式的方式觀看。

本書係儲存了超過一千個的小圖示，可供用作一圖庫，或當成靈感來源。所有的圖表係會被儲存在隨書免費附贈的光碟片上 (Mac 及視窗版)，而且亦可立即應用至專業級印刷媒體和網頁設計上。該圖像亦可用來製作風景明信片 — 不論是列印在紙張上或數位式 — 或用來修飾您的信件，廣告傳單等。

它們係能從光碟片中直接地輸入至大多數的裝置，影像處理軟體，圖式，文字處理裝置和電子郵件等軟體內；不需要進行安裝。有一些軟體程式係可讓您直接存取圖像；而使用其他的軟體時，您可能必須先產生一個文件檔然後才能輸入圖像。請參考您的軟體操作手冊中的說明。光碟片中的檔案名稱係可對應至書上的圖像編號。此光碟片係隨書免費附贈的，而且不得分開販售。假使該光碟片和您的系統並不相容，出版商將不需承擔任何責任。

對於非專業級應用程式，可免費使用單一圖像。所有的圖像皆不得使用於任何類型的商業用途或其他的專業級應用程式上 — 包括所有類型的印刷品或數位式出版品 — 除非事先獲得 Pepin Press/Agile Rabbit Editions 的書面授權。

有關授權和費用方面請洽詢:
mail@pepinpress.com
傳真號碼： +31 20 4201152

page number　　　　　　　　　　　　　　　　　　　　　　　　　　　　中文

本書のミニアイコンは、Palm やその他の PDA（携帯情報端末）等のハンドヘルド オ　ガナイザにお使いいただくためにデザインされたものです。この種の端末の制約から、デザイナーは工夫を凝らして最少ピクセル数でもユーザーがすぐに認識できるような図柄をデザインしています。その結果、シンプルながら、小さくてもすぐにそれとわかるアイコンができあがりました。本書に提供された一千以上のミニアイコンは、グラフィックのリソースとして、ご自分のアイディアで自由にお使いください。イラストはすべて付属の無料 CD-ROM（Mac と Windows 用）に収納されており、そのまま高品質印刷や Web ページデザインにお使いいただくことができます。また、ポストカード（はがきやデジタルポストカード）の図案や、便箋やチラシなどのイラストにもご活用ください。

これらの画像は、CD から直接様々なプログラムにインポートして加工したり、デザインやイラスト、ワープロ、電子メールプログラムに取り込むことも可能です。インストールの必要はありません。一部のプログラムからは直接画像にアクセスすることが可能です。また、プログラムによっては、最初に文書を作成した上で、そこに画像をインポートする必要があります。これらの手順については、各ソフトウェアマニュアルをご覧ください。CD-ROM のファイル名には、本書の画像番号を当てています。CD-ROM は本書に無料添付されるもので、個別販売は行っていません。発行者は、CD がお使いのシステムに対応していなくても、一切責任を負うものではありません。

非商業目的のアプリケーションには、単　画像を無料でお使いいただくことができます。ペピン・プレス/アジャイル・ラビット・エディションズの事前許可を得ない限り、商業目的または営利目的のアプリケーション（あらゆる種類の印刷とデジタルパブリケーションを含む）への使用は認められません。

使用許可と料金に関するお問い合わせ先：
mail@pepinpress.com
Fax +31 20 4201152

日本語

page number

pda planning
priority coc

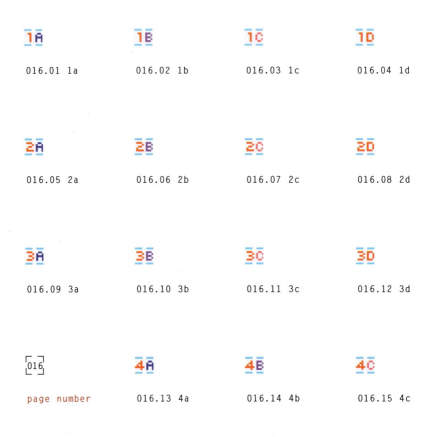

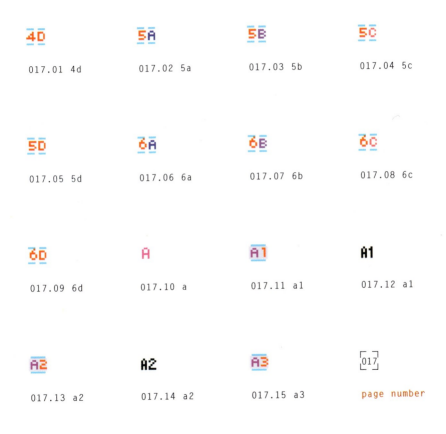

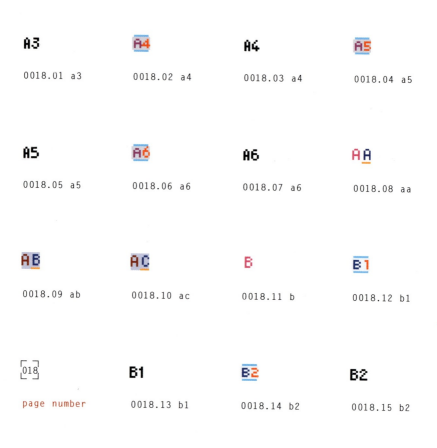

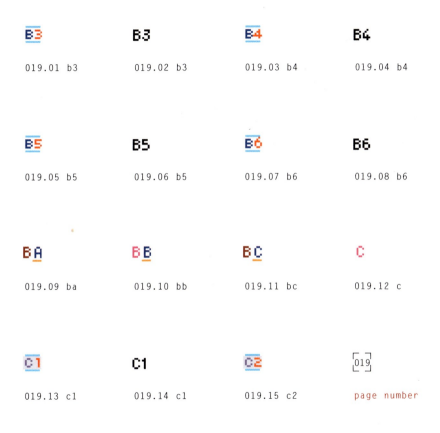

C2	**C3**	**C3**	**C4**
020.01 c2	020.02 c3	020.03 c3	020.04 c4
C4	**C5**	**C5**	**C6**
020.05 c4	020.06 c5	020.07 c5	020.08 c6
C6	**C A**	**C B**	**C C**
020.09 c6	020.10 ca	020.11 cb	020.12 cc
[020]	**D**	**D1**	**D1**
page number	020.13 d	020.14 d1	020.15 d1

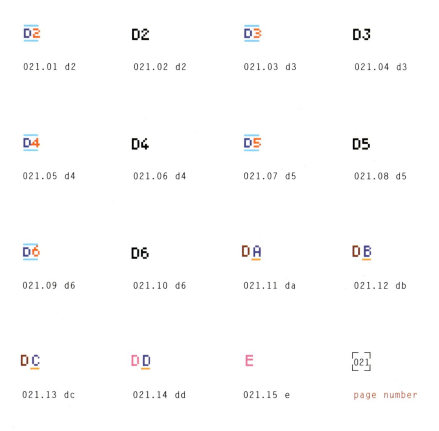

E<u>A</u>	E<u>B</u>	E<u>C</u>	E<u>E</u>
022.01 ea	022.02 eb	022.03 ec	022.04 ee
F	F<u>A</u>	F<u>B</u>	F<u>C</u>
022.05 f	022.06 fa	022.07 fb	022.08 fc
F<u>F</u>	G	G<u>A</u>	G<u>B</u>
022.09 ff	022.10 g	022.11 ga	022.12 gb
[022]	G<u>C</u>	G<u>G</u>	H
page number	022.13 gc	022.14 gg	022.15 h

HA	**HB**	**HC**	**I**
023.01 ha	023.02 hb	023.03 hc	023.04 i
IA	**IB**	**IC**	**II**
023.05 ia	023.06 ib	023.07 ic	023.08 ii
J	**JA**	**JB**	**JC**
023.09 j	023.10 ja	023.11 jb	023.12 jc
K	**KA**	**KB**	[023]
023.13 k	023.14 ka	023.15 kb	page number

kc	L	La	Lb
024.01 kc	024.02 l	024.03 la	024.04 lb
Lc	m	ma	mb
024.05 lc	024.06 m	024.07 ma	024.08 mb
mc	mm	n	na
024.09 mc	024.10 mm	024.11 n	024.12 na
[024]	nb	nc	nn
page number	024.13 nb	024.14 nc	024.15 nn

O	OA	OB	OC
025.01 o	025.02 oa	025.03 ob	025.04 oc
OO	P	PA	PB
025.05 oo	025.06 p	025.07 pa	025.08 pb
PC	PP	Q	QA
025.09 pc	025.10 pp	025.11 q	025.12 qa
QB	QC	QQ	[025]
025.13 qb	025.14 qc	025.15 qq	page number

R	R<u>A</u>	R<u>B</u>	R<u>C</u>
026.01 r	026.02 ra	026.03 rb	026.04 rc
S	S<u>A</u>	S<u>B</u>	S<u>C</u>
026.05 s	026.06 sa	026.07 sb	026.08 sc
T	T<u>A</u>	T<u>B</u>	T<u>C</u>
026.09 t	026.10 ta	026.11 tb	026.12 tc
[026]	T<u>T</u>	U	U<u>A</u>
page number	026.13 tt	026.14 u	026.15 ua

u**b**	u**c**	v	v**a**
027.01 ub	027.02 uc	027.03 v	027.04 va
v**b**	v**c**	w	w**a**
027.05 vb	027.06 vc	027.07 w	027.08 wa
w**b**	w**c**	w**w**	x
027.09 wb	027.10 wc	027.11 ww	027.12 x
x**a**	x**b**	x**c**	[027]
027.13 xa	027.14 xb	027.15 xc	page number

Y	YA	YB	YC
028.01 y	028.02 ya	028.03 yb	028.04 yc
YY	Z	ZA	ZB
028.05 yy	028.06 z	028.07 za	028.08 zb
ZC	ZZ		
028.09 zc	028.10 zz		

[028]

page number

pda planning symbols

[029]

page number

**Art Center College Library
1700 Lida Street
Pasadena, CA 91103**

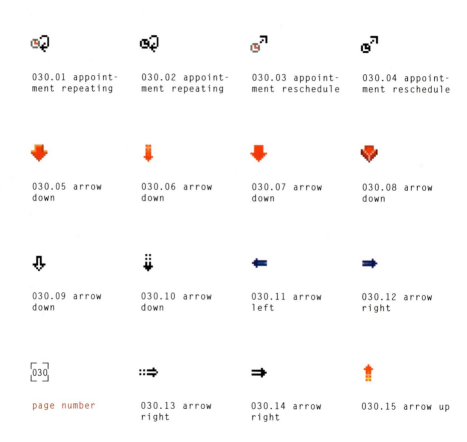

032.01 deadline

 032.02 delegated task

 032.03 giving direction

 032.04 group action

 032.05 group action

 032.06 in progress

 032.07 in progress

 032.08 long term goal

 032.09 long term goal

 032.10 mission statement

 032.11 mis - client server connected

 032.12 mis - client server connected

 page number

 032.13 mis - server not connected

 032.14 mis - helpdesk

 032.15 mis - helpdesk

033.01 mis - information

033.02 mis - information

033.03 mis - network down

033.04 mis - network down

033.05 mis - network up

033.06 mis - network up

033.07 mis - server down

033.08 mis - server restart

033.09 mis - staff meeting

033.10 mis - video conference

033.11 mis - video conference

033.12 mis

033.13 planning beta testing

033.14 planning beta testing

033.15 planning bug fixing

page number

034.01 planning bug fixing

034.02 planning critical path

034.03 planning critical path

034.04 planning critical task

034.05 planning critical task

034.06 planning deadline

034.07 planning deadline

034.08 planning desk research

034.09 planning documentation

034.10 planning filing

034.11 planning issues

034.12 planning issues

page number

034.13 planning overall

034.14 planning overall

034.15 planning progress report

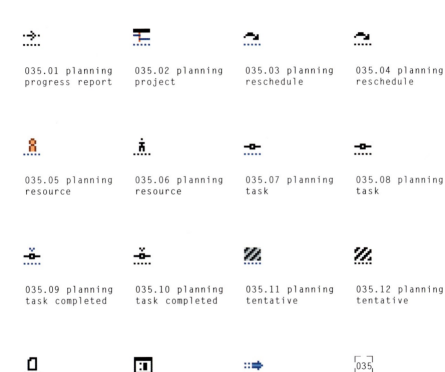

036.01 plan forward 　036.02 planning 　036.03 planning 　036.04 planning

036.05 prioritized daily task 　036.06 prioritized daily task 　036.07 priority list 　036.08 priority list

036.09 project planning 　036.10 report 　036.11 synchronisation 　036.12 synchronisation

page number 　036.13 tentative 　036.14 tentative 　036.15 tentative

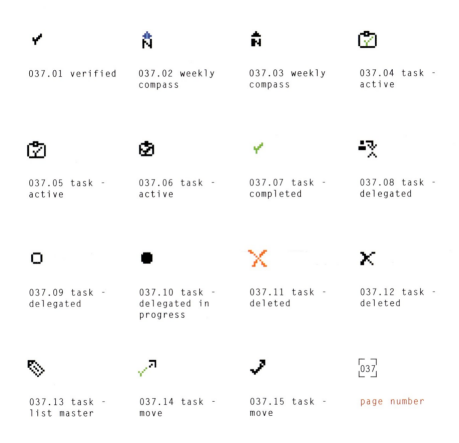

038.01 task - repeating

038.02 task - repeating

[038]

page number

pda planning miscellaneous

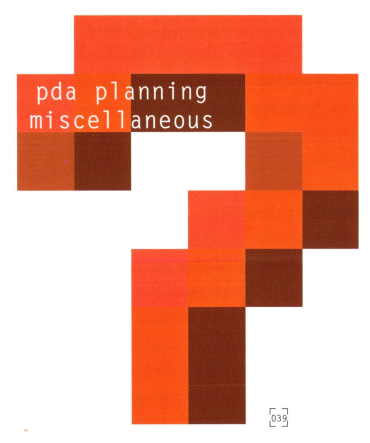

040.01 banner

040.02 banner

040.03 banner

040.04 banner

040.05 bullet - blue

040.06 bullet - brown

040.07 bullet - green

040.08 bullet - darkgreen

040.09 bullet - light blue

040.10 bullet - light green

040.11 bullet - olive

040.12 bullet - orange

page number

040.13 bullet - pink

040.14 bullet - purple

040.15 bullet - red

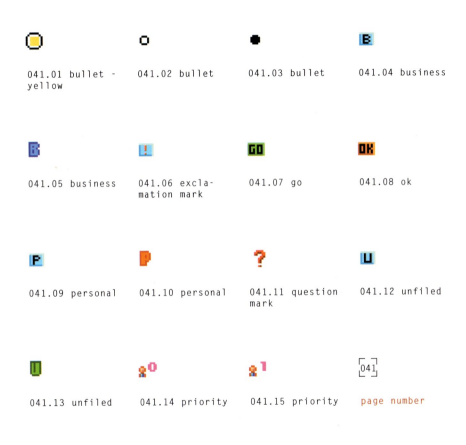

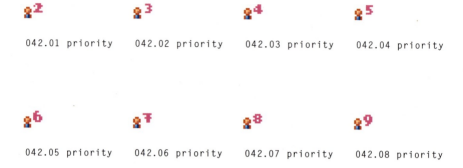

042.01 priority   042.02 priority   042.03 priority   042.04 priority

042.05 priority   042.06 priority   042.07 priority   042.08 priority

page number

office
people

044.01 appointment in office

044.02 appointment in office

044.03 appointment out of office

044.04 appointment out of office

044.05 appointment presentation

044.06 delegate

044.07 delegate

044.08 dinner appointment

044.09 feedback

044.10 feedback

044.11 file project

044.12 interview

page number

044.13 meeting at the office

044.14 meeting budget

044.15 meeting budget

046.01 meeting strategy

046.02 meeting strategy

 046.03 meeting video conference

046.04 meeting video conference

 046.05 meeting

046.06 meeting

046.07 moving

046.08 moving

 046.09 office in

046.10 office out

046.11 personal meeting

046.12 personal online

 page number

 046.13 personal send mail

046.14 personal speech

 046.15 personal staff meeting

048.01 write report

    048.02 write report

050.01 adobe acrobat

050.02 at sign

050.03 calculator

050.04 cd-rom

050.05 cd-rom

050.06 close

050.07 computer

050.08 computer

050.09 computer

050.10 computer

050.11 envelope

050.12 envelope

page number

050.13 envelope international

050.14 fax machine

050.15 file

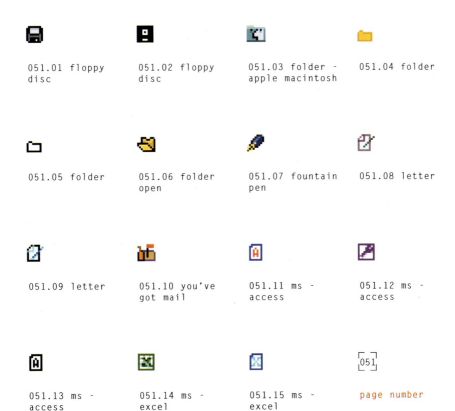

052.01 ms - excel

052.02 ms - windows

052.03 ms - word

052.04 ms - word

052.05 ms - word

052.06 ms - frontpage

052.07 ms - internet explorer

052.08 ms - outlook 2000

052.09 ms - outlook express

052.10 ms - outlook

052.11 ms - project

052.12 ms - visio

page number

052.13 office drink

052.14 palm

052.15 palm

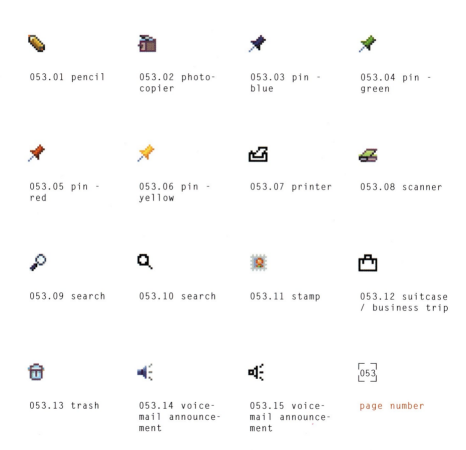

053.01 pencil
053.02 photocopier
053.03 pin - blue
053.04 pin - green
053.05 pin - red
053.06 pin - yellow
053.07 printer
053.08 scanner
053.09 search
053.10 search
053.11 stamp
053.12 suitcase / business trip
053.13 trash
053.14 voice-mail announcement
053.15 voice-mail announcement

page number

page number

business

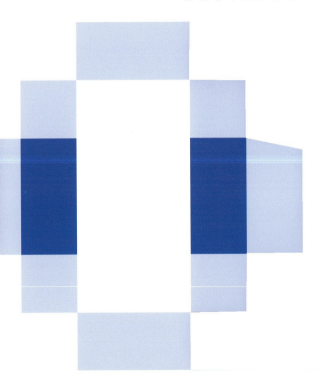

number

056.01 cc - cirrus

056.02 cc - eurocard

056.03 cc - eurocard

056.04 cc - maestro

056.05 cc - mastercard

056.06 cc - mastercard

056.07 cc - visa

056.08 cc - visa

056.09 credit-card

056.10 credit-card

056.11 dollar

056.12 dollar

[056]

page number

056.13 dollar

056.14 dollar

056.15 euro

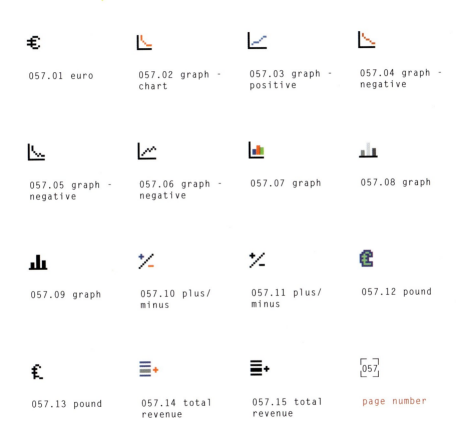

057.01 euro

057.02 graph - chart

057.03 graph - positive

057.04 graph - negative

057.05 graph - negative

057.06 graph - negative

057.07 graph

057.08 graph

057.09 graph

057.10 plus/minus

057.11 plus/minus

057.12 pound

057.13 pound

057.14 total revenue

057.15 total revenue

page number

058.01 yen   058.02 yen

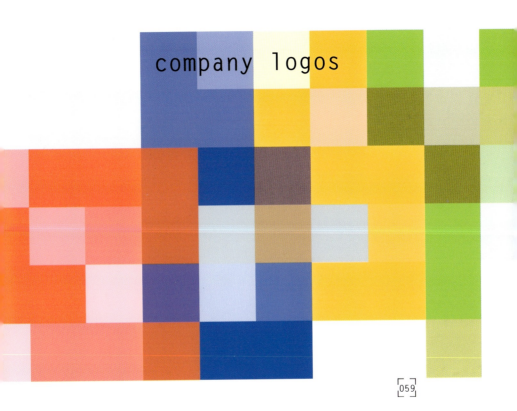

company logos

060.01 adobe

060.02 adobe

060.03 advantage

060.04 air canada

060.05 air france

060.06 air france

060.07 altavista

060.08 america west

060.09 american airlines

060.10 american airlines

060.11 apple

060.12 apple

page number

060.13 apple

060.14 at&t

060.15 avis

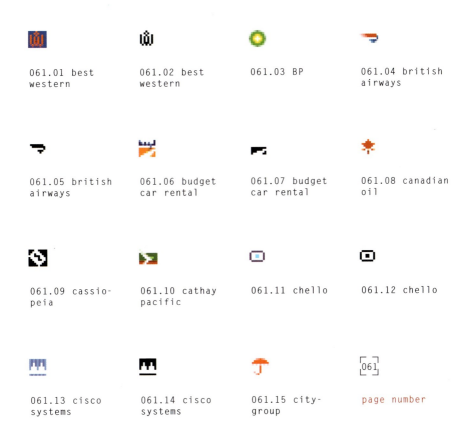

061.01 best western

061.02 best western

061.03 BP

061.04 british airways

061.05 british airways

061.06 budget car rental

061.07 budget car rental

061.08 canadian oil

061.09 cassiopeia

061.10 cathay pacific

061.11 chello

061.12 chello

061.13 cisco systems

061.14 cisco systems

061.15 citygroup

page number

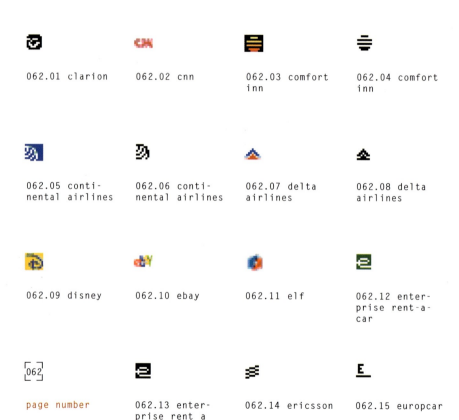

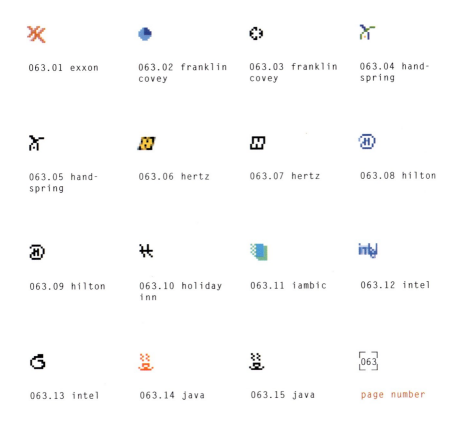

064.01 klm - royal dutch airlines

064.02 klm - royal dutch airlines

064.03 lexington services

064.04 linux

064.05 linux

064.06 lufthansa

064.07 lufthansa

064.08 marriott

064.09 marriott

064.10 microsoft

064.11 microsoft

064.12 mitsubishi

[064]

page number

064.13 motorola

064.14 msn butterfly

064.15 msnbc

065.01 napster 065.02 napster 065.03 national airlines 065.04 national

065.05 national 065.06 netscape 065.07 netscape 065.08 north west airlines

065.09 payless 065.10 pepsi cola 065.11 pimlico software 065.12 quick-time

065.13 radisson 065.14 real-one 065.15 shell page number

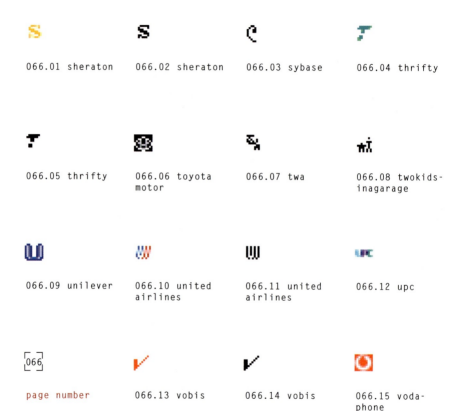

066.01 sheraton   066.02 sheraton   066.03 sybase   066.04 thrifty

066.05 thrifty   066.06 toyota motor   066.07 twa   066.08 twokids-inagarage

066.09 unilever   066.10 united airlines   066.11 united airlines   066.12 upc

page number   066.13 vobis   066.14 vobis   066.15 vodaphone

067.01 winzip   067.02 wyndham   067.03 x org   067.04 x org

067.05 xerox   067.06 yahoo!   067.07 yahoo!

[067]

page number

[068]

page number

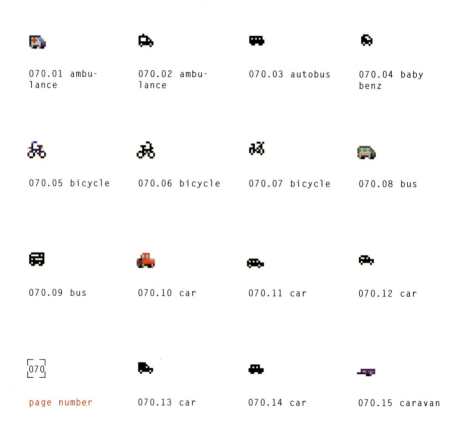

070.01 ambu-
lance

070.02 ambu-
lance

070.03 autobus

070.04 baby
benz

070.05 bicycle

070.06 bicycle

070.07 bicycle

070.08 bus

070.09 bus

070.10 car

070.11 car

070.12 car

070 page number

070.13 car

070.14 car

070.15 caravan

 071.01 fire brigade chief

 071.02 fire engine

 071.03 fire engine

 071.04 fire engine

 071.05 garbage truck

 071.06 gas station

 071.07 gas station

 071.08 glider

 071.09 helicopter

 071.10 jeep

 071.11 jeep

 071.12 locomotive

 071.13 locomotive

 071.14 locomotive

 071.15 locomotive

 page number

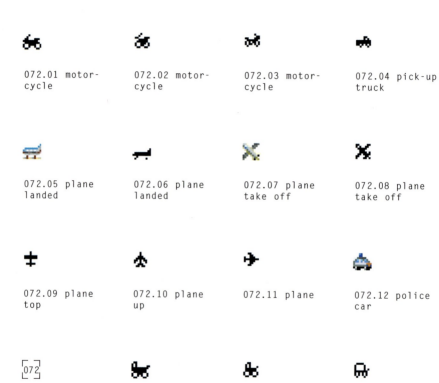

072.01 motor-cycle

072.02 motor-cycle

072.03 motor-cycle

072.04 pick-up truck

072.05 plane landed

072.06 plane landed

072.07 plane take off

072.08 plane take off

072.09 plane top

072.10 plane up

072.11 plane

072.12 police car

page number

072.13 pram

072.14 pram

072.15 pram

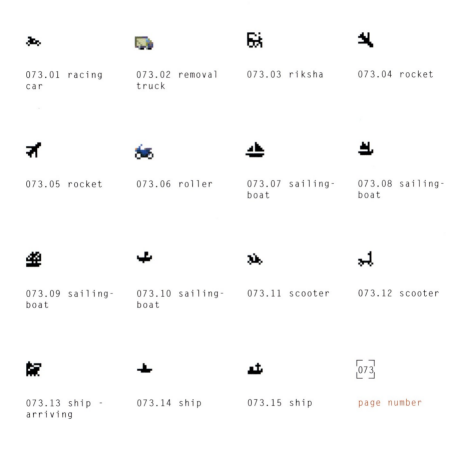

073.01 racing car

073.02 removal truck

073.03 riksha

073.04 rocket

073.05 rocket

073.06 roller

073.07 sailing-boat

073.08 sailing-boat

073.09 sailing-boat

073.10 sailing-boat

073.11 scooter

073.12 scooter

073.13 ship - arriving

073.14 ship

073.15 ship

page number

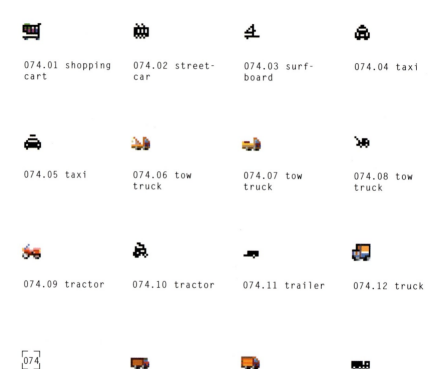

074.01 shopping cart
074.02 streetcar
074.03 surfboard
074.04 taxi
074.05 taxi
074.06 tow truck
074.07 tow truck
074.08 tow truck
074.09 tractor
074.10 tractor
074.11 trailer
074.12 truck

page number
074.13 truck
074.14 truck
074.15 truck

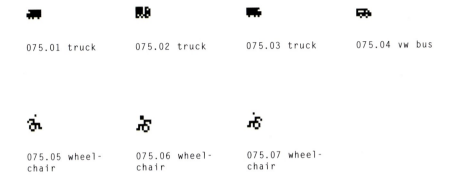

075.01 truck

075.02 truck

075.03 truck

075.04 vw bus

075.05 wheel-chair

075.06 wheel-chair

075.07 wheel-chair

page number

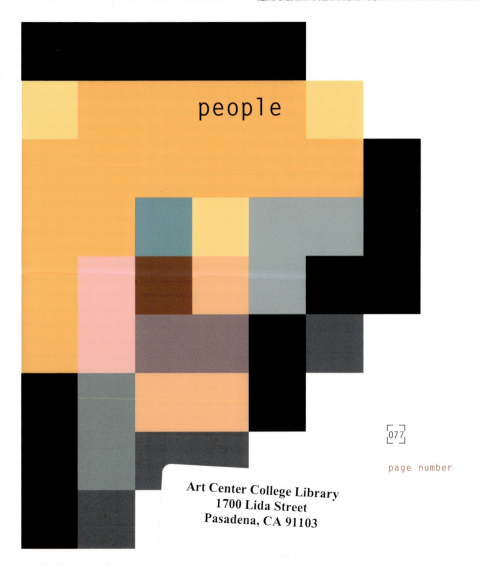

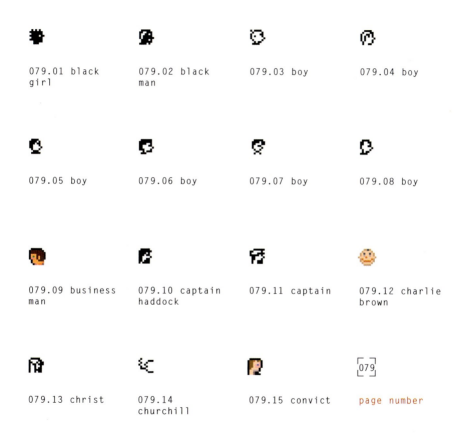

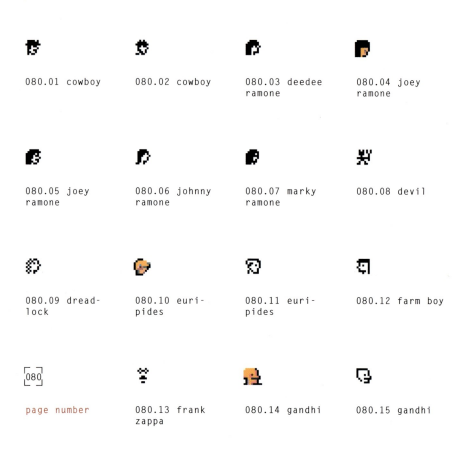

080.01 cowboy

080.02 cowboy

080.03 deedee ramone

080.04 joey ramone

080.05 joey ramone

080.06 johnny ramone

080.07 marky ramone

080.08 devil

080.09 dreadlock

080.10 euripides

080.11 euripides

080.12 farm boy

page number

080.13 frank zappa

080.14 gandhi

080.15 gandhi

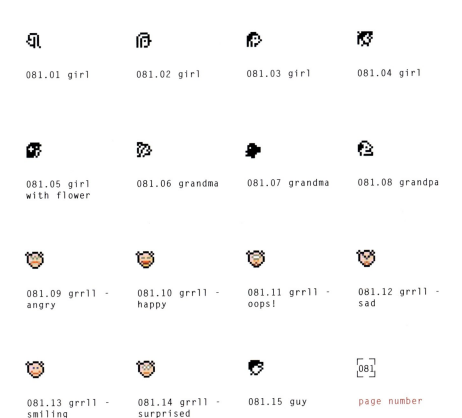

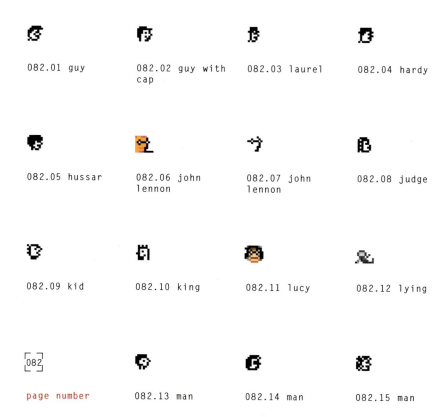

082.01 guy

082.02 guy with cap

082.03 laurel

082.04 hardy

082.05 hussar

082.06 john lennon

082.07 john lennon

082.08 judge

082.09 kid

082.10 king

082.11 lucy

082.12 lying

page number

082.13 man

082.14 man

082.15 man

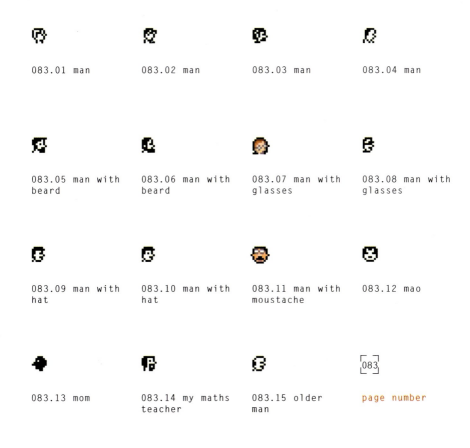

083.01 man

083.02 man

083.03 man

083.04 man

083.05 man with beard

083.06 man with beard

083.07 man with glasses

083.08 man with glasses

083.09 man with hat

083.10 man with hat

083.11 man with moustache

083.12 mao

083.13 mom

083.14 my maths teacher

083.15 older man

page number

084.01 person

084.02 queen beatrix

084.03 rastafarian

084.04 ray charles

084.05 ray charles

084.06 rockabilly

084.07 rockabilly

084.08 roy orbison

084.09 running

084.10 salvador dali

084.11 salvador dali

084.12 screaming

page number

084.13 sister

084.14 sitting

084.15 skinhead

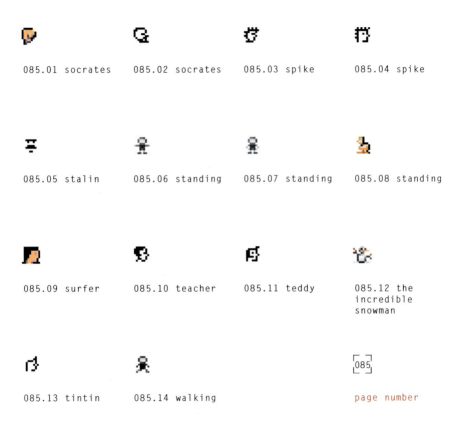

page number

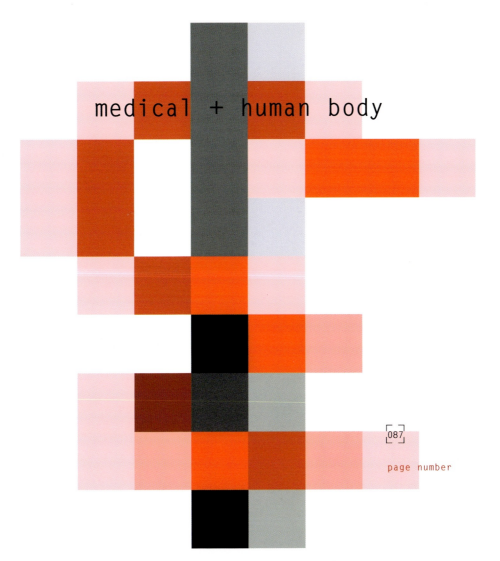

088.01 aaaah!

088.02 aesculapius staff

088.03 blood

088.04 bowels

088.05 dentist visit

088.06 doctor

088.07 ear

088.08 electrocardiogram

088.09 emergency room

088.10 eye

088.11 female sexual organs

088.12 foot

page number

088.13 glasses

088.14 glasses

088.15 glasses

 089.01 h2o

 089.02 hand

 089.03 heart

 089.04 heart

089.05 hospital

 089.06 human body

 089.07 human body

 089.08 immune / lymph system

 089.09 kidney

 089.10 liver

 089.11 lungs

 089.12 male sexual organs

 089.13 medical insurance

 089.14 medical test

 089.15 medication

page number

090.01 medication

090.02 microscope

090.03 nervous system / nerve cell

090.04 nuclear / radiology

090.05 operating room

090.06 organ donation

090.07 pediatrician

090.08 pill

090.09 pill

090.10 potion

090.11 red cross

090.12 respiratory tract

page number

090.13 skin

090.14 stethoscope

090.15 stomach

091.01 surgical mask   091.02 syringe   091.03 tooth   091.04 vitamine drink

page number

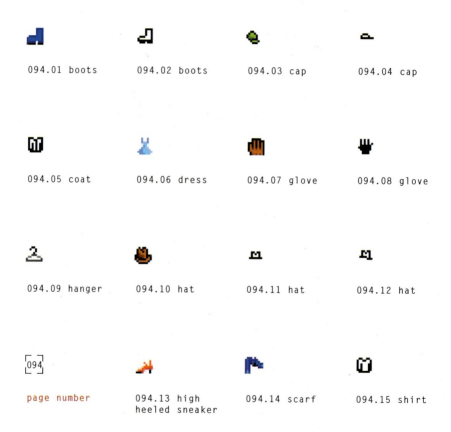

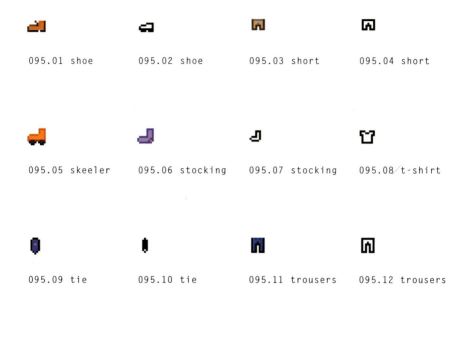

095.01 shoe   095.02 shoe   095.03 short   095.04 short

095.05 skeeler   095.06 stocking   095.07 stocking   095.08 t-shirt

095.09 tie   095.10 tie   095.11 trousers   095.12 trousers

page number

page number

food + drinks

[097]

page number

098.01 apple

098.02 apple

098.03 banana

098.04 banana

098.05 beer bottle

098.06 birthday cake

098.07 birthday cake

098.08 bottle and glass

098.09 bottle and glass

098.10 bottle and glass

098.11 cake

098.12 cake

page number

098.13 cherries

098.14 chicken wing

098.15 chopsticks

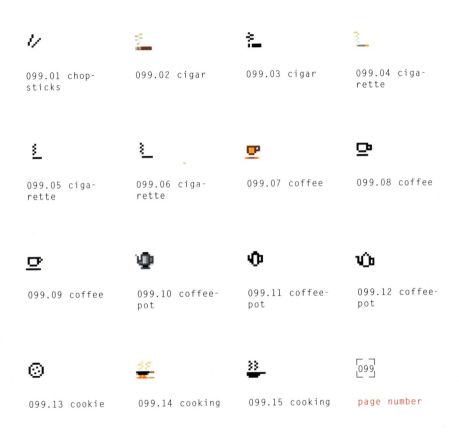

099.01 chopsticks
099.02 cigar
099.03 cigar
099.04 cigarette
099.05 cigarette
099.06 cigarette
099.07 coffee
099.08 coffee
099.09 coffee
099.10 coffeepot
099.11 coffeepot
099.12 coffeepot
099.13 cookie
099.14 cooking
099.15 cooking
page number

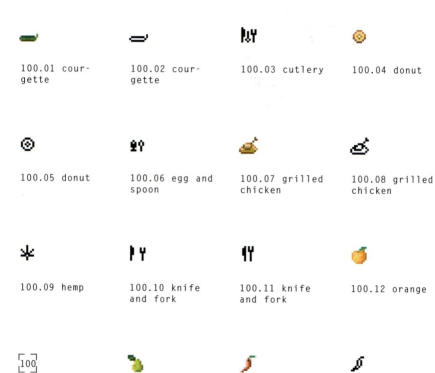

100.01 courgette

100.02 courgette

100.03 cutlery

100.04 donut

100.05 donut

100.06 egg and spoon

100.07 grilled chicken

100.08 grilled chicken

100.09 hemp

100.10 knife and fork

100.11 knife and fork

100.12 orange

page number

100.13 pear

100.14 pepper

100.15 pepper

104.01 bull

 104.02 bunny

 104.03 canadian woodpecker

 104.04 cat

 104.05 cock

 104.06 crab

 104.07 doggy

 104.08 dolphin

 104.09 dolphin

 104.10 duck

104.11 elephant

 104.12 fish

 page number

 104.13 fish

 104.14 godzilla

 104.15 grass-hopper

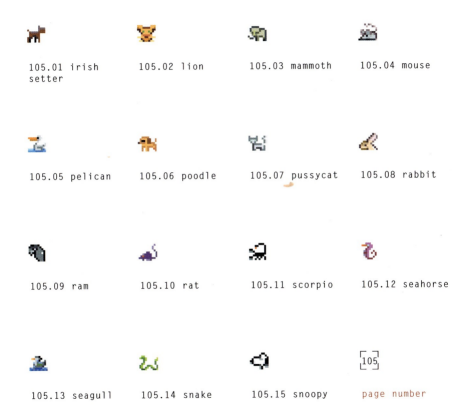

106.01 squirrel   106.02 turtle   106.03 wood-
                                    stock

sports

108.01 american football

 108.02 archery

 108.03 baseball

 108.04 baseball

 108.05 basketball

 108.06 basketball

 108.07 boxing glove

108.08 boxing

 108.09 car racing / carting

 108.10 chess

108.11 chess - bishop

 108.12 chess - king

 page number

 108.13 chess - knight

108.14 chess - pawn

 108.15 chess - queen

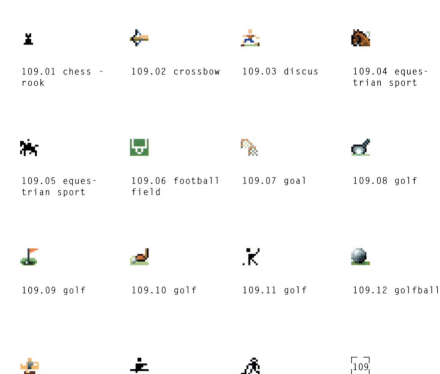

109.01 chess - rook
109.02 crossbow
109.03 discus
109.04 equestrian sport
109.05 equestrian sport
109.06 football field
109.07 goal
109.08 golf
109.09 golf
109.10 golf
109.11 golf
109.12 golfball
109.13 gymnastics
109.14 gymnastics
109.15 hockey
page number

110.01 kick-off

110.02 number one

110.03 number one

110.04 racing flag

110.05 running - jogging

110.06 shooting

110.07 shooting

110.08 skating

110.09 skating

110.10 skiing

110.11 soccer

110.12 soccer

page number

110.13 soccer-player

110.14 stop-watch

110.15 stop-watch

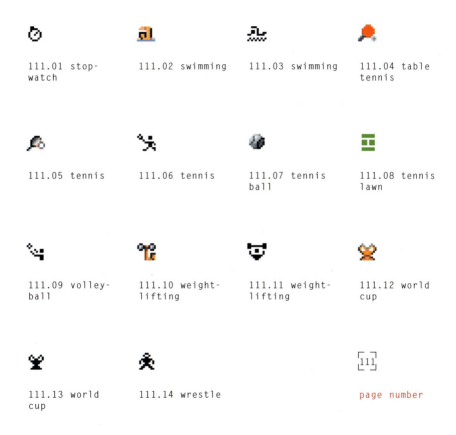

page number

playing cards

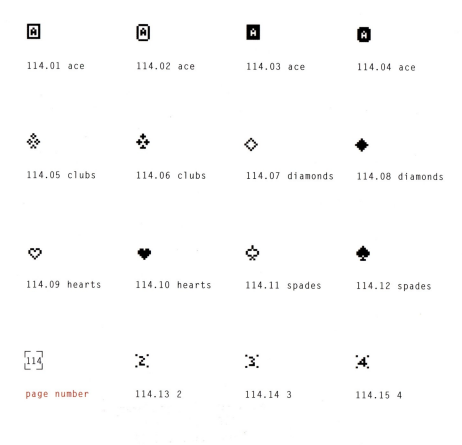

115.01 5

115.02 6

115.03 7

115.04 8

115.05 9

115.06 jack

115.07 jack

115.08 queen

115.09 queen

115.10 king

115.11 king

page number

Art Center College Library
1700 Lida Street
Pasadena, CA 91103

page number

astrology + astronomy

118.01 aquarius

118.02 aries

118.03 cancer

118.04 capricorn

118.05 gemini

118.06 leo

118.07 libra

118.08 pisces

118.09 sagittarius

118.10 scorpio

118.11 taurus

118.12 virgo

[118]

page number

118.13 chinese sign - bull

118.14 chinese sign - dog

118.15 chinese sign - dragon

119.01 chinese sign - horse

119.02 chinese sign - lion

119.03 chinese sign - monkey

119.04 chinese sign - pig

119.05 chinese sign - rabbit

119.06 chinese sign - rat

119.07 chinese sign - snake

119.08 chinese sign - turtle

119.09 chinese sign - rooster

119.10 jupiter

119.11 mars

119.12 mercury

119.13 moon

119.14 neptune

119.15 pluto

page number

♄	☉	⛢	♀
120.01 saturn	120.02 sun	120.03 uranus	120.04 venus

122.01 adoration

122.02 angel

122.03 bible study

122.04 buddha

122.05 buddha

122.06 buddha

122.07 candle

122.08 candle

122.09 candle-menora

122.10 cathedral

122.11 celtic cross

122.12 chandelier

page number

122.13 christmas night

122.14 christmas tree

122.15 christmas tree

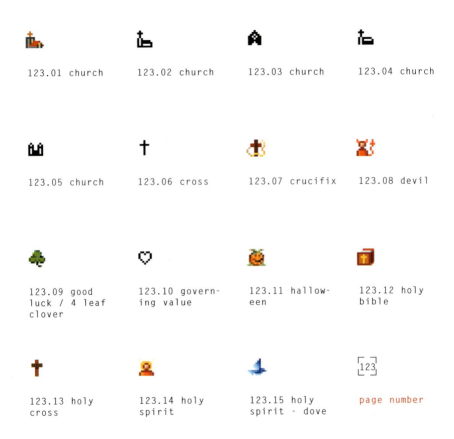

123.01 church
123.02 church
123.03 church
123.04 church
123.05 church
123.06 cross
123.07 crucifix
123.08 devil
123.09 good luck / 4 leaf clover
123.10 governing value
123.11 halloween
123.12 holy bible
123.13 holy cross
123.14 holy spirit
123.15 holy spirit - dove
page number

124.01 incense

 124.02 ixthus

 124.03 jesus

 124.04 joined prayer

 124.05 monk

 124.06 mosque

 124.07 pax christi

 124.08 peace

 124.09 prayer

 124.10 praying hands

124.11 praying hands

 124.12 russian orthodox church

page number

 124.13 sermon

 124.14 star

 124.15 star of david

125.01 tombstone   125.02 tombstone   125.03 yin-yang   125.04 yin-yang

page number

general

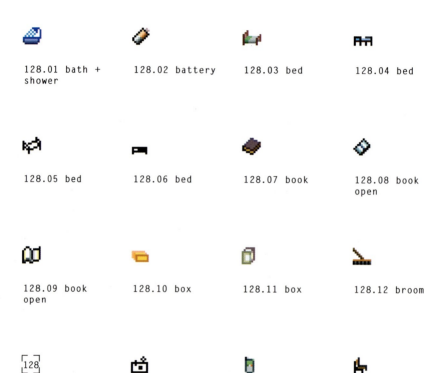

128.01 bath + shower
128.02 battery
128.03 bed
128.04 bed
128.05 bed
128.06 bed
128.07 book
128.08 book open
128.09 book open
128.10 box
128.11 box
128.12 broom
page number
128.13 camera
128.14 cell-phone
128.15 chair

129.01 cleaning
129.02 clock
129.03 clock
129.04 construction
129.05 construction
129.06 couple
129.07 cupboard
129.08 danger
129.09 dustpan
129.10 dustpan
129.11 electric drill
129.12 electrical plug
129.13 filling knife
129.14 film camera
129.15 flag - france

page number

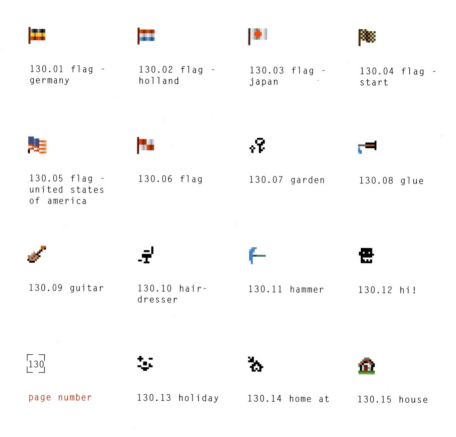

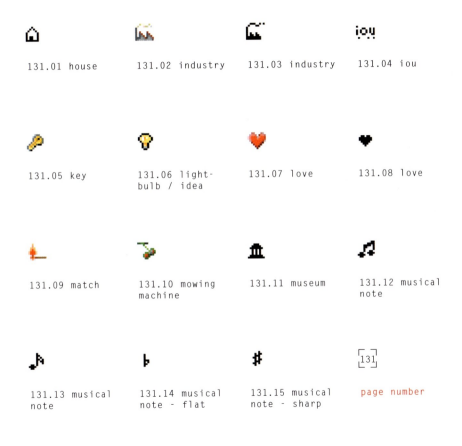

132.01 musical note - f clef

132.02 musical note - g clef

132.03 office building

132.04 office building

132.05 padlock

132.06 paint-roller

132.07 paint-brush

132.08 party!

132.09 perfume bottle

132.10 perfume bottle

132.11 person - appointment

132.12 person - at the dentist

page number

132.13 person - backpack

132.14 person - carrying/moving

132.15 person - conversation

 133.01 person - excuse me

 133.02 person - methinks

 133.03 person - monologue

 133.04 person - presentation

133.05 person - reading

 133.06 person - speech

133.07 person

 133.08 pliers

 133.09 present

 133.10 present

133.11 rake

 133.12 sanding machine

 133.13 saw

 133.14 saw

133.15 saw

 page number

134.01 scissors

 134.02 scissors

 134.03 screw-driver

 134.04 sewing

 134.05 soldering gun

 134.06 speech balloon

 134.07 speech balloon

 134.08 spray

 134.09 spray

 134.10 stapler

 134.11 suitcase

 134.12 suitcase

 page number

 134.13 table

 134.14 table

 134.15 telephone

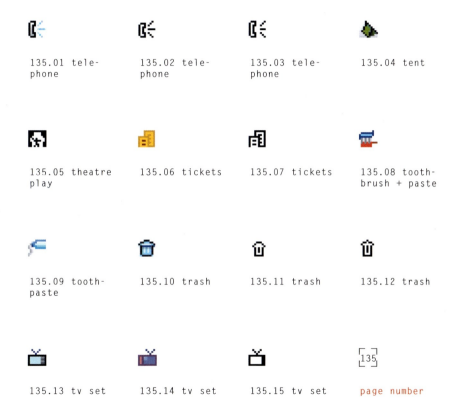

136.01 vacuum cleaner

136.02 video cassette

136.03 washing machine

136.04 washing machine

136.05 water tap

136.06 weather fog

136.07 weather moonlit night

136.08 weather rain

136.09 weather snow

136.10 weather snowflake

136.11 weather starry night

136.12 weather sunny

page number

136.13 weather waterloo sunset

136.14 weather wind

136.15 weather partly clouded

Art Center College Library
1700 Lida Street
Pasadena, CA 91103